The Eiffel Tower

Bernard Marrey, *Architectural historian*

A strange destiny befell this tower, chosen to be the "star attraction" of a temporary exhibition, but rapidly to become a symbol of Paris and one of the most universally celebrated monuments. This is doubly strange because the project, initially turned down by its constructor, Gustave Eiffel (he found it lacking allure), became the most frequented monument in Paris after Notre Dame Cathedral (free entry) less than one century later, with more than six million visitors annually. It is even stranger as this monument—a "first" without strictly speaking being a technical exploit—never inspired emulation, even though the 1,000-foot-high tower fueled every engineer's dream, and other companies had the technical capacity to build as high, if not higher. Yet it was necessary to wait until 1930 for a New York skyscraper, the Chrysler Building, to exceed it, by 18 metres.

Then several elements came together: an ambitious entrepreneur, Eiffel; a savvy politician and skilled communicator, Édouard Lockroy; and

an exceptional political regime, finally and really democracy. Now, although often considered technically outmoded, the Eiffel Tower still retains all its attraction.

The political and economic context

In late 1884, with the Third Republic having been in power just ten years, the government decided to organize a universal exhibition for 1889. Why so early? The last exhibition, that of 1878, had been mounted in haste for political reasons. After a humiliating defeat in 1871 [following the Franco-Prussian War, 1870], elections brought a Monarchist majority into the Chamber of Deputies whose division had permitted the instauration of a Republic using a round-about means of an amendment in 1875. Ensuing elections brought about a Republican majority in 1877 which, in an attempt to efface the memory of defeat and to rally the country around a Republican ideal, decided on an exhi-bition for the year 1878. But with only one short year to prepare, its success was mediocre and, by the end of the 1878 exhibition, a celebration with great fanfare for the centenary of the French Revolution was promised. The Republicans kept their promise, all the more so since the Republic had not proven itself: the first had quickly turned to a dictatorship and the second had been thrown over at the end of three years by a coup d'État. There had not been a Republican regime in Europe and, in France, the ruling classes were in the majority hostile to the idea. The Republic, led by the middle class, soon failed the working classes who

La République, executed after a proposal by the Morice brothers, winners of the competition organized by the City of Paris in 1879, to erect a monument to the glory of the Republic. The statue was inaugurated on the Place de la République on 14 July 1883.

Award-winning projects by Soitoux and Granet, *L'Illustration,* 25 October 1879.

found support in the rather colourless General Boulanger. Indeed the country was entering into "one of the gravest depressions which had ever marked the history of an industrialised nation". France slipped from second to fourth rank of industrial powers and would not escape the crisis until the mid-1890s. The causes of this economic crisis were multiple: demographic stagnation, a drop in agricultural productivity, the phylloxera epidemic in 1876, poor orientation of investments directed toward foreign rather than domestic markets, and weakening of the banking system after the crash of the Union Générale in January 1882. Perhaps, too, should be added the

Boulangist agitators in front of the premises of *La Cocarde,* March 1888.

egoism of the bourgeoisie who, having come to power, had no intention of allowing the working classes to benefit from it, a fact which did not stimulate demand.

The governments attempted to bring about solutions. Compulsory education by March 1882 was a good way to curb the crisis, at least in the lumber industry, by multiplying orders for school furniture, and in building, by launching the construction of numerous lycées and university faculties. But the general ambience was worse than morose. At the social level, statistics showed that the agricultural population decreased from 51 per cent in 1875 to 45 per cent in 1891, and that the Senate refused to outlaw child labour for those under thirteen until 1892.

Metal construction

Metal construction began to develop during the eighteenth century. Its expansion in France was slowed down by Revolutionary and Imperial wars (during which metal was applied for other purposes) and by coal shortages in the country. By the early 1800s, allied to progress in the glass industry wherein France took the lead, metal became ubiquitous in covered arcades, warehouses, and workshops, permitting both an increase of space by limiting the number of structural columns and an augmentation of natural lighting to a considerable degree.

Napoleon III's choice of metal for Paris's central food markets in 1853 corresponded not only to the prince's desire but to that of the public, hostile to a stone or "fortified hall". Very soon, every French town had its own metal market place. In Paris, the concentration of commerce gave rise to the *grand magasins* [department stores], each of which, after the Le Coin de Rue in 1864, was arranged around a central concourse illuminated by a glass and metal cupola. However, metal construction was linked foremost to rail-

Iron or steel

Wrought iron is an alloy of iron and carbon consisting of between 2 to 6 per cent carbon. It is malleable, slightly flexible, brittle, and very resistant to crushing. Steel is an alloy of iron and carbon containing from 0.3 to 1.8 per cent carbon. Forged or rolled iron is situated between the two: stronger and less brittle than wrought iron, it resists flexion and extension quite well.

Wrought iron was first employed as a support (pillar, column), then, but with more difficulty, in construction work where it was rapidly replaced, by the 1840s, with rolled iron (angle bars, I- or T-sections) and by sheet metal. Invented by Henry Bessemer in 1856, steel did not start to be utilised in French civil construction until the early twentieth century, for reasons of its cost, consumption of coal (of which France was impoverished), and difficulties inherent in the phosphorus content of Lorraine iron. In 1900, France produced 590,000 tons of steel. The Eiffel Tower is an iron structure.

Section through the Palais de l'Industrie, drawing by Max Berthelin (Paris, Musée d'Orsay). Erected for the Universal Exposition of 1855, it was the work of engineer Alexis Barrault.

Gare Saint-Lazare, by Claude Monet (1840-1926), oil on canvas, 1877 (Paris, Musée d'Orsay).

way expansion during the 1850s and 1860s which, after a slow-down, had experienced a sudden new revival with Charles de Freycinet's arrival in 1877 to the Ministry of Public Works. To stimulate the economy, this graduate of the École polytechnique, a major Parisian engineering school founded by Napoleon I, initiated the plan to provide port ameni-

ties and construct 16,000 kilometres of railway track. In a period when road transport was nonexistent, his aim was to render the poor regions less isolated so as to permit them to develop their own products. This project was heralded by all metal construction companies, from the most powerful such as Fives-Lille et Cail, Compagnie des Batignolles, and Schneider, to the lesser ones as well, including Daydé & Pillé, Baudet-Donon-Roussel, Moisant, and Eiffel.

The Eiffel firm

Gustave Eiffel had established his firm in 1867. Born into a middle class Dijon family in 1832, he graduated from the École centrale, chemistry division. Soon after graduation, he met Charles Nepveu, a specialist in construction on difficult terrain. The Pereire brothers [train and real estate developers, and financiers] had commissioned him to construct the Bordeaux Bridge over the River Garonne, a

Gustave Eiffel at around 35 years of age (Paris, Collection Tour Eiffel).

particularly delicate operation due to shifting sediments, force of the tidal bore, and the necessary cantilevering of the bridge. Nepveu commissioned Eiffel to oversee the construction site. At a mere twenty-six years of age, Eiffel completed the project to everyone's satisfaction in less than two years (1858-1860). Eiffel next directed various construction sites and carried out brokerage work until 1867, year of the second

Construction of the Pont de Bordeaux, where bridge piers were sunk with compressed air (Paris, Collection Tour Eiffel).

Universal Exposition when he associated with Théophile Seyrig, a fellow Centralien graduate, ten years his junior. Seyrig assured technical direction, Eiffel commercial and general matters. As such, they constructed a certain number of bridges and viaducts, including the Maria Pia Bridge at Porto, the result of an 1875 international competition. In 1878, Seyrig broke off rela-

Construction of the Maria Pia Bridge, on the River Douro, Portugal (Paris, Collection Tour Eiffel).

tions with Eiffel, who subsequently confided the design office to Maurice Koechlin, a graduate of the Polytechnical School of Zurich.

But Eiffel had secured the commission for the vestibule entry and domes of the Universal Exposition of 1878: 3,000 tons of beams. If his firm executed structures for religious and civil architecture in Paris and New York—the Rue des Tournelles Synagogue, the Church of Notre-Dame-des-Champs, Le Bon Marché Department Store, and the Statue of Liberty, amongst others—it worked mostly for railway companies, principally those of the Pereire brothers, either in France (for example, the Compagnie du Midi) or abroad, notably in Spain, Portugal, and Hungary.

Statue of Liberty, with its metal structure achieved by Ets. Eiffel (Paris, Collection Tour Eiffel).

The 300-metre tower

Eiffel and his collaborators (Maurice Koechlin, left) at the Garabit Viaduc base in 1884 (Paris, Collection Tour Eiffel).

Proposal for a 300-metre tower, before the last development stage, with decorative fittings by Sauvestre. The final design would be simplified (Paris, Collection Tour Eiffel).

Birth of a project

In 1884, although the centenary Exposition proposal had not been officially announced, everyone was preoccupied by it and looked for a strong concept capable of attracting public attention. Gustave Eiffel spoke to his engineers in the last days of May. His firm was still under the spell of success over the Garabit Viaduct. On 26 April, the two half-arches of the viaduct, separated at their base by 165 metres, had been joined at the key, 120 metres above the River Truyère, "with almost mathematical precision", as Eiffel reported. In a remote region of the Massif Central, some twenty kilometres south of Saint-Flour, it necessitated dispatching 3,300 tons of metal structure, sustaining, nourishing, and housing about one hundred men and horses, and erecting the immense structure. This construction site thus represented to Eiffel alone a veritable enterprise, and he did not have to rely too heavily on the experience of Émile Nouguier, a methods engineer, to set up the project.

A forty-four year old engineer from the École des mines [National School of Mining Engineering], Nouguier had been hired by Eiffel from Établissements Gouin in 1876. With Maurice Koechlin (who directed the design office), they made a good team despite their age difference. Koechlin was barely twenty-eight in 1884. Originally from Guebwiller in Alsace, he had studied under Karl Culmann, the founder of graphic statics, at the Zurich Polytechnic before working for two years with the Compagnie des

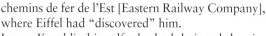

chemins de fer de l'Est [Eastern Railway Company], where Eiffel had "discovered" him.

It was Koechlin himself who had designed the viaduct proposal, reworking and improving upon Seyrig's design for the Maria Pia Bridge. For the struts, he substituted three-sided profiled iron sections to replace the closed caissons, permitting much easier surveillance and maintenance. It was these iron sections that were retained for the tower because, although the bridge was horizontal and the tower vertical, both projects were similar.

Six weeks after the junction of the two Garabit arches, Koechlin and Nouguier signed a conceptual sketch, dated 6 June 1884, showing a 300-metre-high pier for the Exposition of 1889. They proposed it to Eiffel, their employer, who was less than enthusiatic, leaving them free to pursue the study without him. To him, a bridge pier, even though gigantic, hardly seemed attractive.

During the summer of 1884, Koechlin and Nouguier refined their project with the collaboration of Stephen Sauvestre (1847-1919), a fashionable, eccentric architect within a wealthy milieu, before submitting it to Bartholdi, with whom they had worked on the Statue of Liberty. They also showed it to the commissioner of the exhibition of decorative arts scheduled for autumn at the Palais de l'Industrie. He agreed to exhibit the drawing, which the two engineers again showed to Eiffel. The latter hence revised his decision and, on 18 September, deposited a patent under the names Gustave Eiffel, Émile Nouguier, and Maurice Koechlin, "for a novel arrangement to permit the construction of metal piers and pylons to a height capable of exceeding 300 metres".

The Washington Monument, begun in 1848 as a 600-foot (183-metre) obelisk and completed in 1885, only reached 169.25 metres, including the aluminium tip. Neither Nouguier, Koechlin, nor Eiffel knew nothing about any previous projects, at least when they established their tower design. The two highest existing monuments were approximately 170 metres.

Bourdais' sun-column

If Eiffel had changed his mind, it was because Jules Bourdais had just submitted a complete proposal for the Exposition to Maurice Rouvier, Minister of Commerce within Jules Ferry's government. A former Centralien like Eiffel, Jules Bourdais had become an architect, constructing with Gabriel Davioud the Trocadéro Palace for the 1878 Exposition, amongst other works. As such, he had made the acquaintanceship of Charles de Freycinet, Minister of Public Works, whose protégé he had become.

Bourdais' "star attraction" had been a 100-metre sun-column, carried rapidly to 300 metres, undoubtedly to rival Eiffel's concept. The column was to rest on a 66-metre-high base on which rose a tower whose diameter, wider at the pedestal base than the summit, would be on average 28 metres. Towards the

La Mole Antonelliana, in Turin, realised by engineer Alessandro Antonelli (1798-1888), reached 168 metres at its completion in 1900.

Pylon of 300-metres, Émile Nouguier and Maurice Koechlin's preliminary design, 6 June 1884 (Paris, Collection Tour Eiffel).

Patent application, in the names of Eiffel, Nouguier, and Koechlin (Paris, Collection Tour Eiffel).

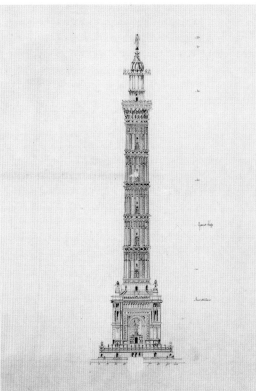

Sun-column, proposal by Jules Bourdais (Paris, Collection Tour Eiffel). In the upper section of the base, Bourdais made provisions for "a comfortable, hygienic hospice for convalescents obliged to leave the city in search of fresh air to restore their health". Such concern may draw a smile today, but it was intended to allay the major objection to the two proposals: the cost of the projects in relation to their inutility.

apex, materials would be more delicate, and might be covered with a revetment in sheet metal or repoussé copper such as used on the Statue of Liberty.

Launching the exposition

In the autumn of 1884, Jules Grévy signed a decree setting the dates for a universal exhibition from 5 May to 31 October 1889. Without waiting to learn more, Eiffel signed a contract on 12 December with Nouguier and Koechlin establishing terms on which he committed himself, in exchange for their patent rights, to cite their names in perpetuity and to pay 1 per cent dues on the preliminary estimate approved by the Director General of the Exposition.

Submitted on 10 March 1885, the commission's report proposed once again the Champ-de-Mars site, defining a construction programme to include an Arts Palace and a Science Palace, destined as permanent buildings, and making a preliminary cost evaluation. Six months later, on 1 August, a law was passed to open a 100,000-franc survey credit. Thus far there was no mention of a tower. One might imagine that Eiffel profited from this year to vaunt his project before the ministries concerned and before the City of Paris. In his general report on the 1889 Exposition, Alfred Picard wrote: "In Eiffel's mind, this colossal work ought to constitute a brilliant manifestation of our country's industrial power, to attest to the immense progress realised in the art of metal construction, to celebrate the unprecedented development of civil engineering during the century, to attract numerous visitors, and to contribute largely to the success of the great, peaceful conferences organized for the 1789 centenary."

In the spring of 1886, the exhibition proposal began to gel after the deputies had voted in the principle by a large majority on 21 April, at the end of stormy debate.

Competition for an iron tower

Two weeks later, on 2 May 1886, Édouard Lockroy, Minister of Commerce and Industry in Freycinet's cabinet, launched a competition whose goal was "to facilitate a comparison and thereby extrapolate the best option to adopt". Possible sites were enumerated, as were necessary surfaces. The material was also chosen: "Principal buildings will be erected entirely in iron with infill of brick, masonry, staff, and the like." However, in the ninth article, the ruling stipulated: "Competitors should study the possibility of raising on the Champ-de-Mars a 300-metre-high iron tower with square base, 125 metres on each side. They will draw up this tower on the plan of the Champ-de-Mars and, if they deem it suitable, they may present another plan without the said tower." Not only had the tower become an integral part of the programme but, in imposing iron as the material, it ruled out Bourdais' sun-tower, despite Charles de Freycinet's protection. Even stranger still was the precise mention of a square-based tower with 125-metre sides. One cannot help thinking that the minister had already made up his mind.

Édouard Lockroy

Édouard Lockroy was the son of an actor and author of comedies and vaudeville. At twenty, he enlisted himself with Garibaldi and, after his victory in unifying Italy, became secretary to Renan, then Alexandre Dumas before publishing scathing articles against Napoleon III in Le Figaro. In 1869, he teamed up with Victor Hugo's two sons, Charles and François, who co-founded (with several others) the Republican journal Le Rappel. Shortly thereafter he was condemned to a four-month jail sentence for anti-government attacks. He presented himself in the elections of 8 February 1871, won a seat in Paris, and attempted, unsuccessfully, to avoid the rupture between the Commune and the government at Versailles. Imprisoned, he was released without sentence in June 1871. Elected the following month to the Municipal Council of Paris, he then led a double career as a journalist and Republican politician.
In 1877, Lockroy wed Charles Hugo's widow. Upon Victor Hugo's death on 22 May, he was given

Édouard Lockroy, deputy for Paris, drawn by Mars (1827-1891). Minister of Commerce and Industry in the Freycinet government, he was the State's representative on the Eiffel Tower project.

Lockroy surely remembered the success of Giffard's balloon at the 1867 and 1878 expositions. Lashed down in the court of the Tuileries Gardens, outside the official festivities, it had provided the real "star attraction". The 25,000m³-balloon, rising to 600 metres, allowed 35,000 people to discover Paris from 18 July to 4 November 1878.

responsibility for the poet's funeral by the Minister of the Interior. But his opposition to a religious internment caused him to be judged too far to the left and led to his being placed on the sidelines of the committee of national unity. Nevertheless Lockroy played an active role in the organization of this day. Nothing proves that he sensed there the advantage that a politician could reap from the symbolic force of a popular demonstration, but it is evident that this ceremony touched him very profoundly.

Seven months later, on 7 January 1886, the prospective President of the Council, Charles de Freycinet, offered him the Ministry of Commerce, to which he requested be joined with Industry, a portfolio he held until 30 May 1887.

The choice

If Lockroy leaned in favour of Eiffel's proposal, to the point of taking up his specified materials and dimensions within the competition rules, it was surely because of the modernity of iron and the renown

Award-winning project by Eiffel and Stephen Sauvestre, competition for the Universal Exposition of 1889 in Paris, drawing by De Bré, *L'Illustration,* 5 June 1886.

that such a realisation would bring to French builders. In addition, and not without significance, as an entrepreneur, Eiffel would assume most of the financing. Launched on 2 May 1886, the competition was to close on the 18th. From 12 May, Lockroy named a consultative commission of thirteen members, under his presidency, charged with examining the feasibility of Eiffel's project. The commission brought their report to three professors: Édouard Collignon from the École des Ponts et Chaussées [School of Bridges and Highways], Victor Contamin from the École Centrale, and Édouard Phillips from the École Polytechnique who rendered their clear, obviously unanimous, favourable conclusions on 12 June. During this period, the twenty-nine-member jury, also presided over by Lockroy, decided to award twelve of the 107 proposals received, the largest prize (4,000 francs) going to those of Dutert, Eiffel, and Formigé. Article 16 of the rules stipulated that "the Minister of Commerce and Industry himself reserves the absolute right to allocate the award-winning proposals". Ferdinand Dutert obtained the commission for the Galerie des Machines, Jean-Camille Formigé, that of the Palais des Beaux-Arts et des Arts libéraux,

| 17

Ferdinand Dutert's project, first prize, competition for the Universal Exposition of 1889 in Paris, *L'Illustration,* 5 June 1886.

and Eiffel that of the tower. On 6 July, the budget for the exposition was voted in.

Six months later, on 8 January 1887, along with the tenderer Eiffel and prefect Eugène Poubelle, representing the City of Paris, the Minister (simultaneously commissioner-general of the Exhibition) courageously co-signed a convention stipulating that the entrepreneur would commit himself to constructing the tower and rendering it serviceable on the opening day of the exposition. Eiffel received a 1,500,000-franc grant and authorisation to exploit the tower during the entire duration of the exposition, on condition that prices would not exceed 2 francs to mount to the first floor and 5 francs to the third, prices dropping to 1 franc on Sundays. His concession was prolonged for twenty years beginning on 1 January 1890, a time limit after which it reverted to the City of Paris, substituted for the State as proprietor of the monument from the end of the exposition. On 26 January 1887, three weeks after the signature of the agreement, the first pickaxe struck at the foundations.

Project by Cassien-Bernard and Francis Nachon, second prize, competition for the Universal Exposition of 1889 in Paris, *L'Illustration,* 5 June 1886.

18 |

The engineer Eiffel, caricature by Luke, 1889 (Paris, Collection Tour Eiffel). "A vertiginously absurd tower dominating Paris, just like a gigantic, black factory stack with its savage mass overshadowing Notre-Dame, Sainte-Chapelle, the Tour Saint-Jacques, the Louvre, the dome of the Invalides, the Arc de Triomphe, all of our monuments humiliated, all of our architecture belittled, which will vanish in this astounding dream"; from the "artists'" letter of protest, 14 February 1887.

Gustave Eiffel, caricature in *Le Central* (Paris, Collection Tour Eiffel).

"The tower will be the tallest edifice built by man to date. Will it not be grandiose in its fashion? And why would that which is admirable in Egypt become hideous and ridiculed in Paris?" Eiffel's response to the "artists'" protest.

The polemic

On 14 February, *Le Temps* published a letter dubbed "the artists' protest", addressed to Monsieur Alphand, Director of Building Works at the exposition. Written upon the instigation of architects at the Institut de France, furious to see iron triumph and exhibition commissions escape them, the letter was signed by their "pals" at the École des Beaux-Arts, painters then in vogue, everyone from Meissonier to Bouguereau, as well as Gérôme, Bonnat, and Lenepveu, and accompanied by writers such as François Coppée, Sully Prudhomme (Académie Française members), and many others (forty-seven in all) whose names have been lost to history, with the exception of Guy de Maupassant and Charles Gounod. It read:

"As writers, painters, sculptors, architects, and amateurs impassioned by the beauty of Paris, until now intact, we come to protest with all our strength and indignation; in the name of slighted French taste, in the name of art and French history under threat, against the erection of the useless and monstrous Eiffel Tower in the heart of our capital [...]. Will the City of Paris continue to associate itself any longer with such oddity, with the mercantile imagination of a machine constructor, to disfigure itself irreparably and dishonour itself? Because the Eiffel Tower, which even commercial America would not want, is, without any doubt, the dishonour of Paris."

Eiffel's and Lockroy's responses

Following the "artists'" letter, *Le Temps* published Eiffel's reaction: "... The first principle of an architectural aesthetic is that the essential lines of a monument are determined by perfect appropriateness to its end purpose. Now, what conditions had I to consider above all else in the tower? Resistance to wind. Very well! I maintain that the curves of the four arrises of the monument [...] will convey a great impression of strength and beauty; because they will transmit visually a conceptual hardiness in the overall design, just as numerous voids within the construction elements themselves will strongly emphasise the constant concern of not exposing unnecessarily those surfaces, dangerous to the stability of the edifice, to hurricane violence.

"There remains in the colossal an attraction, a particular charm, to which theories of ordinary art are hardly applicable. Does not one support the idea that it is by their artistic value that the pyramids so strongly struck man's imagination? What are they, after all, but artificial hillocks? And yet, what visitor remains unmoved in their midst? Who has not been filled with irresistible admiration? And what is the source of this admiration, if not the immensity of the effort and the grandeur of the result?"

"The tower will possess its own beauty. Just because we are engineers, does one not thus believe that beauty preoccupies us in our constructions and that, at the same time as we make solid and durable [objects], we do not endeavour to create elegance?" Eiffel's response to the "artists".

In his capacity as commissioner of the exposition, Lockroy had published the letter he had addressed to Alphand: "Do not mention to these men that it is unpleasant to see beforehand an attack on the Universal Exposition only

by those who ought to defend it; that a protest signed by names so illustrious will have repercussions in all of Europe and will risk furnishing a pretext to certain foreigners to not participate in our festivities; that it is bad to seek to ridicule a peaceful work to which France attaches itself with even more ardour at the present moment because it sees itself more unjustly suspected from abroad. [...]

What I beg you to do, is to receive and conserve the protest letter. It should be displayed in the cases of the Exposition. Such elegant, noble prose signed by names recognised throughout the world cannot fail to attract crowds and, perhaps, to astonish them."

Architectural beauty and wind resistance, details of the Eiffel Tower's metal structure.

Eiffel Tower foundations, May 1887, engraving. In the distance, the former Trocadéro Palace.

View of a compressed-air caisson, engraving. Section showing subterranean work, access tubes, and earth excavation, as well as masonry construction (Paris, Collection Tour Eiffel).

Adjustment of the beam junction at the first floor by raising the footings, engraving (Paris, Collection Tour Eiffel).

The construction site

The east and south pier foundations were executed by pickaxe, those of the north and west (close to the Seine) by compressed air, the sheet metal caissons being buried 5 metres below water level, the deepest not exceeding 15 metres. The four solid masonry blocks were terminated by 30 June 1887; 30,000m³ of rubble had been evacuated.

Assemblage began on 1 July. The most delicate operation was the erection of four cantilevered pillars and placement of the horizontal beam at the first level. The pillars were to be propped up at a height of 26 metres by wooden scaffolding which also supported the horizontal beam, constructed at the end of each pillar. There remained the connection, two by two, of each of the eight half-beams. This was no longer the two 165-metre half-arches to join, as at Garabit, but four half-beams, each separated by a distance of 104 metres. To this end, a space had been left under the pier shoes in which to introduce an 800-ton hydraulic jack, so as to be able to modify the inclination of the piers and allow the junction of the four half-

Sauvestre, Nouguier, Eiffel, Koechlin, and Salles (left to right) on the tower's first platform (Paris, Collection Tour Eiffel).

Installation of air-compression caissons for the foundations.

Construction phases of the Eiffel Tower

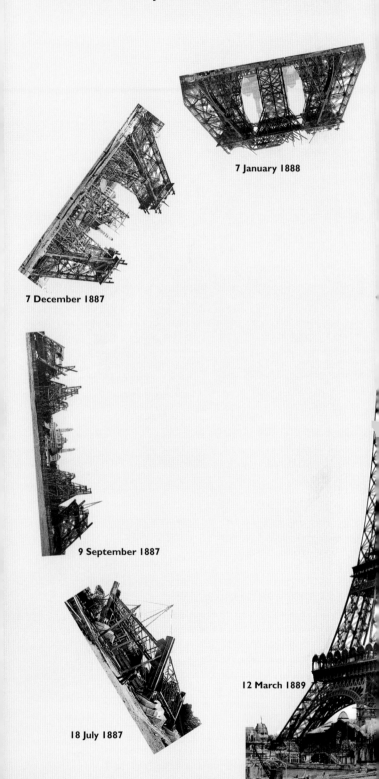

7 January 1888

7 December 1887

9 September 1887

12 March 1889

18 July 1887

from July 1887 to March 1889.

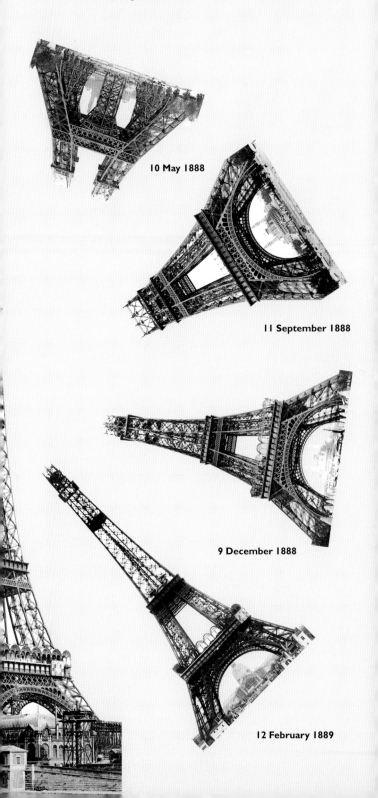

10 May 1888

11 September 1888

9 December 1888

12 February 1889

Gustave Eiffel receives journalists on the construction site, 4 July 1888 (Paris, Collection Tour Eiffel).

beams. The moment that the piers had been rendered interdependent and could be riveted, the jacks were removed, thus accomplishing the most difficult task. It was reported that, on 29 April 1888, Eiffel arranged a celebration to mark the exploit on the platform 57 metres above ground. Assemblage could then continue—not without risk, given the height—but the stone course was assured.

With a crew of 150 workers on average (slightly increased to 200 in the last weeks), assemblage was pursued during exactly twenty-one months. Duration of work was nine hours per day during winter, and thirteen during summer, with no allowance for weekly rest or annual holidays. Essentially labour involved carpenters and erectors; the carpenters, always at the summit, built the temporary platforms on which the erectors worked.

The strike

In the summer of 1888, strikes in the building sector broke out throughout most of France. In September, the tower was approaching its mid-height when, on Monday the 17th, the workers demanded a uniform increase of 20 centimes per hour for the *"mousses"* [jargon for ship's boys or child apprentices], paid 45 centimes per hour, as well as for the carpenters, paid 75 centimes. On 19 September, Eiffel proposed an increase of 5 centimes, accorded only to deserving workers. From the midday pause, a work stoppage was declared; four delegates were elected. Shortly thereafter, they were received by Eiffel and Compagnon, chief of the construction site, who made them new propositions, still far from the original demand and

Twenty-Six Views of the Eiffel Tower, lithographs by Henri Rivière, 1889 (Paris, Musée d'Orsay, Collection Eiffel). *From top to bottom:* workman in the tower; Eiffel Tower construction sites during winter; workman on a beam of the campanile arch.

A highly qualified workforce.

It was said that the tower had been constructed by the *compagnons du tour de France* [reputed French guild of journeymen-carpenters], who had wanted to leave their signatures there in the style of a late "masterpiece". It is certain that a number of Eiffel's skilled workers came from the guilds, but not all, as more than a century after the Le Chapelier law forbidding all workmen's associations, guilds were badly perceived. Nonetheless, there was no doubt about the high qualifications of this labour force, out of which some had already built the Garabit Viaduct, as well as the Maria Pia Bridge in Porto.

Riveters' station, engraving after a photograph. With the aid of pliers, the "pile holder" takes a red-hot rivet from the brazier stoked by a *"mousse"* and introduces it into the hole of the iron girders to join. Rivet edges were enlarged with a hammer, then pounded down with a sledgehammer by a rapper (Paris, Collection Tour Eiffel).

2,500,000 rivets to assemble the 18,000 iron sections.

still selective, whilst the strikers demanded uniform increases, insisting on the fact that dangers incurred were the same for everyone and family expenses similar. The strike was triggered. It is also necessary to add that as winter approached, the length of the day was diminishing, and salaries in proportion to it.

Consent was reached on 21 September on the following basis: 5-centime increase across the board from 1 September; 5-centime increase for strikers only from 1 October; 5-centime increase from the moment duration of work was restricted to nine hours so as to compensate for the diminuation of salary as the passage of the day decreased from ten to nine hours; a 100-franc bonus once the third platform was set in place. These were the terms the delegates had understood, and work recommenced on the Saturday morning of 22 September. Soon after, Eiffel had a notice placarded in which the text differed slightly from that of the first accord. The 5-centime increase calculated from 1 October was to be paid out to personnel working at the summit and no longer to the strikers; compensation for a nine-hour day paid out as ten was omitted. Was this the case of a simple misunderstanding?

No matter what the case, it became the source of a new conflict which exploded on 21 December. On Saturday, a panel hung at the construction site entry warned that workers who did not resume work on that same day would be judged as having quit. Some

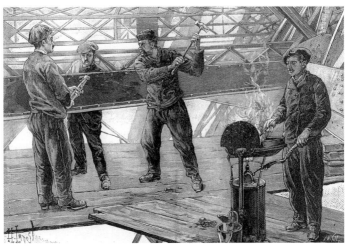

unemployed workers turned up, provoking brawls. Arguments and police interventions ensued. On Sunday, 23 December, the strikers decided to resume work, without their demands having been met. The tower just overshot the 200-metre mark. Temperatures hovered at –10° Centigrade.

View of the erecting cranes functioning up to 150 metres, engraving after a photograph (Paris, Collection Tour Eiffel).

Double crane assuring the lifting of pieces between the second and third floors, engraving after a photograph. Work organization (pieces ready

Organization of the work

To the firm's credit, there were no fatal accidents during work hours, a fact testifying to the good organization of the construction site and the very high degree of expertise of the labour force. At the Champ-de-Mars, all pieces arrived numbered, ready for use, and even partially pre-assembled to avoid all work other than erection. Erectors received the pieces or units which they provisionally assembled with bolts to those sections already mounted. Then, as soon as one unit had been properly constituted, the bolts were replaced by rivets.

A new 12-ton derrick had been conceived specifically by Monsieur Guyenet, an engineer in Eiffel's company, to be able to lift a 3-ton weight. Its charge had been well chosen. Had it been stronger, a heavier block of units could have been lifted, but manoeuvring would have taken longer; less strong, manutentions would have been more numerous. There, too, it was critical to calculate precisely because there were 7,500 tons of iron to lift and no time to waste.

to be used, assemblage and erecting) undoubtedly assisted in avoiding fatalities on the construction site. At the British construction of the gigantic Firth of Forth bridge in Scotland (2,250 metres resting on three piers more than 100 metres high), around one hundred deaths had already occurred by September 1888, that is five years before the inauguration. But at the Forth, untrimmed pieces arrived at the site, adjustments and assembly being carried out in place.

Fireworks display in 1888 on the tower whose second platform had just been terminated.

It was not astonishing that, from this moment, the construction site itself had become a place of attraction. As a journalist noted: "The number of curiosity-seekers increased more and more. Foreigners passing through Paris never missed the opportunity to pay a visit to the colossal enterprise, and all returned home from there wondrous, even a little bit envious."

Inauguration in aid of the Republic

Gustave Eiffel at the top of the tower, 1889 (Paris, Collection Tour Eiffel).

Elections approached in a politically tense climate. Hard times, confiscation of the Republic by a grasping bourgeoisie, and its fragility in face of Empires which threatened it from the exterior all nourished a new Bonapartism in which General Boulanger was its propeller. After having several landslide victories in the provinces, he presented himself in Paris on 27 January 1889. To everyone's surprise, the Left bastion toppled, giving Boulanger 245,336 votes against 162,875 to the moderate radicals. It was time to retaliate. The Minister of the Interior, Ernest Constans, put a strategem into place which fully succeeded with Eiffel's backing. The inauguration of the tower was previewed for the same day as the exposition, on 6 May, afternoon of the anniversary of the opening of the Estates General in 1789. But time was pressing. An "intimate" celebration on the construction site had also been organized for Sunday, 31 March, with the Municipal Council, around fifty guests, and the press. That same day, Constans received a friend of General Boulanger. Excusing himself for several minutes, he left on the top of his desk, as though inadvertently, an order to arrest Boulanger two days later. Alerted to the fact, the General escaped to Belgium on 1 April. This precipitous, hurried departure, which in normal times would have made headlines in all the papers, was eclipsed by the tower's inauguration.

Inauguration of the Eiffel Tower, 31 March 1889 (Paris, Collection Tour Eiffel). Gustave Eiffel hoists the tricolour flag to the tower summit. A few years later, Pierre de Coubertin recalled: "When the flag fluttered on the tower, when the scaffolding disappeared and, in the resplendent gardens, water in the fountains began to flow, everyone knew that in Paris reality had surpassed the dream."

General Boulanger eclipsed by the Eiffel Tower, caricature in *Le Pilori,* July 1889.

The 1,710 steps were climbed up by twenty or so courageous men, the remainder of the procession tapering along the road. Eiffel raised the flag (7.5 by 4.5 metres) and a banner offered by the workers. A twenty-one-gun salute was fired from a fireworks box. By 2:40pm, a speech was delivered, champagne was poured. Descending to the foot of the tower, Eiffel received the rosette of an officer of the Legion of Honour, presented by Tirard, President of the Council.

The lifts

What remained to be completed were the lifts, a difficult problem as hydraulic lifts were then in the earliest stages of development. The first French lift had been presented by Léon Édoux at the Universal Exposition of 1867. But the problem posed by the ascension of the tower, due to its height and pier inclinations, was without precedent. A call for tenders put three companies and three systems into competition:

• Roux, Combaluzier & Lepape constructed two inclined lifts called "articulated pistons" which linked the ground to the first floor within the east and west piers.

• Otis (even though foreign, as no French company had accepted the risk) installed lifts in the north and south piers to serve the second floor with traction via pulley-block cables and hydraulic press.

• Édoux guaranteed transport from the second floor to the summit by a double lift with two equilibrated cars. One car was pushed by a hydraulic piston, the other, providing the counterbalance, was joined to it with two flat cables. Mid-way, an intermediary platform

Édoux lift,
1889 Exposition, drawing by Carlowski, *Un voyage à la Tour Eiffel* (Paris, Bibliothèque nationale de France).

Opposite page
Roux-Combaluzier & Lepape lift,
east and west pillars.

allowed the transfer of visitors from one car to the other. The cable-suspended car was equipped with a parachute system. The double lift assured a service during ninety-four years, with a minimum consumption of energy.

The Roux-Combaluzier & Lepape lift transported ninety persons at a speed of 60 metres per minute from ground to first floor; Otis lifts, forty-two persons at 120 metres per minute from the first to second floors; and the Édoux double lift, sixty-five persons at 54 metres per minute from the second floor to the summit.

1082

Entry to the Universal Exposition of 1889, by Jean Béraud (1849-1936), oil on canvas (Paris, Musée Carnavalet).

Success

Popular success was instantaneous. Out of a total record of more than 32 million visitors to the exposition (compared with 16 million during 1878, only just 10 million in Philadelphia during 1876, and 7 million in Vienna during 1873), 1,968,287 visitors went up the tower. It is difficult to tell if they were more attracted to the tower than they were to the exposition itself.

Even before work was terminated, in order to administer the tower, Eiffel founded the Société de la Tour Eiffel with the Banque Franco-Égyptienne, the Société Générale, and the Crédit Industriel et Commercial on 31 December 1888, with a capital of 5,100,000 francs. It was to this company that exposition visitors contributed a total of 5,919,844 francs. With diverse concessionary products, restaurants, and the like, takings mounted to

Allegory to the glory of the centenary of the French Revolution (Paris, Collection Tour Eiffel).

Overall view of the Universal Exposition of 1889 in Paris, taken from the Esplanade des Invalides, coloured engraving, *L'Illustration.*

6,500,000 francs. Construction costs had risen to 7,400,000 francs and operating costs to one million francs. The City of Paris having voted in a grant of 1,500,000 francs, the operation almost broke even from the first year, the next twenty years brought in a profit, even drastically reducing maintenance costs and personnel.

Such success made everyone forget the risks taken by Eiffel. For example, just as work was about to begin, a neighbour brought legal action against the State and the City lest the tower (or pieces thereof) fall onto his property. Awaiting the outcome of this action would have slowed down the work. Eiffel undertook eventual damages for the State and City, assuming all

Le Figaro Exposition, 1889 (Paris, Musée d'Orsay, Eiffel Collection).

Souvenir from the Universal Exposition of 1889 (Paris, Collection Tour Eiffel).

Visitors to the first floor of the Eiffel Tower. Americans came in canoes, Italians on bicycles (through the Alps), a mujik by foot, three Viennese in a wheel-barrow .... Easter Monday was the busiest day, with 23,202 visitors; September 9, the day of the highest takings, 60,756 francs. It was impossible to meet the demand of all those seeking to ascend via the lifts.

risks and perils at his own costs. From that moment, "entrepreneur" was no longer a pejorative term, and to those who wonder why the tower was not named after its two inventors, it is legitimate to underscore that Eiffel had to assume the multiple roles of salesman, animator, administrator, and organiser in order to complete the project. The exploit would not have been feasible without the conjunction of a strong personality—master of a superbly organized enterprise, ready to take double-or-nothing risks—and a dangerously unstable political situation. Faced with the domestic upheaval due to the Boulangist movement, with foreign danger of the Triple Alliance between

**Eiffel Tower
ablaze,
Exposition
of 1889,**
engraving by
Georges Garen
(Paris, Musée
d'Orsay, Eiffel
Collection).

**Night festivities
at the Universal
Exposition
of 1889,**
painting by Roux
(Paris, Musée
Carnavalet).

Austria, Germany, and Russia (to which the Italian realm rallied), the French Republic (upholding the message of 1789) wanted to bring to the world, and to Europe in particular, the proof of its strength and peaceful intentions. In an epoch when man was still riveted to the earth, the tower exploit was comparable to the first Sputnik in 1957. There also existed the same desire to break with diplomatic isolationism (no foreign head of state came to celebrate the centenary of the French Revolution), the same willingness to demonstrate to the world the excellence of the regime.

At night, the tower was illuminated with hundreds of gas jets protected by opaline globes. On the last

**The Eiffel
Tower in ice
at Saint-
Petersburg,**
engraving (Private
Collection).

**Franco-Russian
fetes in Paris,**
fireworks display
seen from the
Eiffel Tower, *Petit
Journal* illustrated
supplement (Paris,
Collection Tour
Eiffel).

floor, two beacons mounted on a circular railing alternatively swept the city in a circumference of 10 kilometres, whilst from higher still, in the campanile, a beacon sent out three signals in blue, white, and red every ninety seconds. Such success bred envy. Every city wanted its own tower, but every project failed except three. The most rapid was Saint Petersburg, where a 60-metre Eiffel Tower in ice was built in 1890. In Lyon, a private society constructed the 80-metre-high Fourvière Tower in 1893, based on the plans of E. Colonges, built on a 372-metre hill. Two years later, Blackpool (a small seaside resort in Lancashire, England) erected a 158-metre tower in an amusement park.

The tower after 1889

The tower and science

If Eiffel had been more cautious than Bourdais in uses envisaged during different phases of the project, he had nonetheless mentioned meteorological and astronomical observations. Once the tower was achieved, he did not relent until he found a scientific justification, already envisaged at the end of his concession. That preoccupied him more than his implication in the Panama affair which led him to transform the company (registered under his name) into an anonymous firm entitled Ateliers de Construction de Levallois-Perret and to confine its direction to his son-in-law, Adolphe Salles. In 1893, the latter was to be condemned, at the same time as Ferdinand de Lesseps, despite their notoriety, for breach of trust. He appealed the decision and the judgement was quashed on 15 June on grounds that the statute of limitations had been exceeded.

On the advice of his friend Éleuthère Mascart, Director of the Bureau Central Météorologique, Eiffel had Richard Frères install an observatory on the tower, together with measurement apparatuses on various levels. In 1890, he installed another apparatus within his property at Bruyères in Sèvres, then at the Villa Salles in Beaulieu in 1901, at the Château de Vacquey near Bordeaux in 1902, and his Ploumanach villa in Brittany in 1906.

Eiffel perfected multiple measurement methods, executed new apparatuses such as the heliographic recorder, and published diverse books on his work. In 1906, he drew up the first meteorological atlas compiling graphics of daily, monthly, seasonal, and annual values observed in twenty-five French stations. The universal success of this publication led him to update it for the next seven years.

Perhaps disappointed by the lack of practical meteorological results, or attracted by the specific study of wind, his old enemy, Eiffel became personally implicated in aerodynamics, a new science which he helped to found with Ludwig Prandtl. In 1903, he installed a shoring on the tower's second-floor platform which he called the "belfry" from which a cable descended to the ground. Weights of various sizes were dropped down the cable length, and air resistance measured. A clever mechanism assured automatic breaking several metres above ground. Measurement of the fall was thereby obtained, on condition that there was no wind.

In extreme circumstances, this system would have sufficed for metal construction purposes, but the development of aeronautics convinced Eiffel that it was necessary to reverse the methodology and act directly on the wind. It was therefore the object that became immobile. It was placed under a measuring instrument

Research on gravity at the second-platform laboratory, engraving (Paris, Collection Tour Eiffel).

(which aerodynamicists call a "scale"), and one varied the air force that was blown over it. Such measurements had been attempted in various countries with little success. Eiffel next constructed a ventilating fan on the Champ-de-Mars at the very foot of the tower. Inaugurated in the spring of 1909, it functioned for two years, during the course of which he experimented with nineteen airplanes and several dirigibles. Tatin, Blériot, Farman, Voisin, and other constructors came there to carry out tests. Having ceded a part of the Champ-de-Mars area to residential real estate developers, the City of Paris demanded the removal of these testing sheds. Eiffel was obliged to move, profiting from the occasion to install an improved ventilating fan at no. 67, Rue Boileau, in Auteuil [16th arrondissement of Paris], where it is still located. Then seventy-nine years old, he directed it for another ten years, assisted solely

Santos-Dumont in a dirigible, *Petit Parisien* illustrated supplement (Paris, Collection Tour Eiffel).

Aerodynamic ventilating fan laboratory in the Rue Boileau, Paris.
Gustave Eiffel holding a model airplane conceived by Victor Tatin. In 1917, with Louis Breguet, Eiffel perfected the L.E., an airplane endowed with monoplane aerofoils without shrouds, which constituted an innovation (Paris, Collection Tour Eiffel).

by two engineers recruited from the Ateliers de Levallois. At eighty-nine years of age, he requested the Ministry of Air to designate his successor. Eiffel died two years later in 1923, aged ninety-one.

The tower and audiovisuals

It was another science, however, that saved the tower from probable demolition upon expiry of the concession on 1 January 1910. On 8 May 1902, the eruption of Mount Pelée destroyed Saint-Pierre-de-la-Martinique, together with the cable linking the island of Guadeloupe. Charged by the army with questions regarding wireless telephones, Captain Ferrié re-established communications via the wireless, thereby demonstrating its utility. Upon his return to France, he came up with the idea of exploiting the tower. Terribly pleased by the opportunity, on 15 December 1903, Eiffel

Experiment with wireless communications on the tower's third floor.
The first wireless communication between the Eiffel Tower and the Pantheon was carried out by Eugène Ducretet in October 1898. Here shown, Ernest Roger, Ducretet's collaborator (Paris, Collection Tour Eiffel).

Use of the tower for the wireless telegraph during the 1914-1918 war.
Les Vingt-Cinq Ans de la tour Eiffel [Twenty-Five Years of the Eiffel Tower], coloured engraving, Petit Journal illustrated supplement, 1914 (Paris, Collection Tour Eiffel).

The tower during German occupation.
Adolf Hitler on the esplanade of the Palais de Chaillot.

announced to the Minister of War his desire to put the tower at Ferrié's disposal. The engineering office accepted his offer on 24 January 1904 "under the reservation that there would be no expenses involved", and, from the following year, installations ceded by Eiffel permitted, in all weather conditions, to assure communications with fortified towns to the east. In 1907, contact was established with Bizerte. On January 1909, Victor Colin and Maurice Jeance carried out preliminary wireless experiments for the navy. Several months later, the military radio-telegraph station left its sheds for an underground installation at the tower base.

From that moment, the tower was saved. Concession was extended until 1 January 1926 "for reasons of the useful work that was made there". Nevertheless, the Société d'exploitation de la Tour was obliged to pay a 5,000-franc licence fee to the City of Paris to which a charge proportional to revenues was added.

In 1910, the tower sent out its first regular transmission of hourly signals, at night perceived at 5,200 kilometres, at daytime at half that distance. It became possible to create an international time organization which unified the measurement of time worldwide and determined longitudes with exactitude. During the course of the summer of 1915, the first transatlantic contacts were established between the Eiffel Tower and Arlington, Virginia. At a shorter distance, such communications allowed contact to be maintained with aircraft responsible for protecting Paris and, eventually, to intercept enemy messages. It was in this way that the notorious Mata Hari was identified as a spy.

On 6 February 1922, the first news transmissions were diffused from a gardener's barracks camped at its base, followed by the first radiophonic concerts. Maurice Privat presented his first daily programme, a spoken journal, on 3 November 1925, from 6 to 7 o'clock in the evening. On 26 April 1935, the tower transmitted the very first television emission (60 lines) from a studio installed on the Rue de Grenelle at the initiative of Georges Mandel, Minister of the

| 41
First radio
transmissions
diffused from
the tower;
Sacha Guitry,
Yvonne Printemps,
and General Ferrié
in 1921 (Paris,
Collection
Tour Eiffel).

PTT [Post, Telephone, and Telegraph Company]. Definition progressed to 455 lines from 31 March 1939, and spectators at the Marigny Theatre discovered an image of Louis Jouvet in *Knock*.

During the Occupation, enjoined by the administrative staff to render tower installations inoperable, the tower management cut the lift cables and demounted some electric devices. Like Paris, the tower remained plunged in darkness. Occupying Germans forbade visits, except for its troops, which had to climb up by foot. Like France, the tower was liberated in August 1944, and its transmitter requisitioned by the American army. Television production resumed by March 1945 and, in 1947, Gilles Margaritis launched circus programmes in 455 lines. In November 1948, lineage passed to 819 and, by September 1949, a daily journal was diffused. Programmes then increased. In 1956, a fire in the transmission premises destroyed the tower summit. A new platform was installed in 1957, endowed with an antenna which culminated at 320.75 metres. In 2000, a new antenna extended the tower height to 324 metres.

New television antenna at the Eiffel Tower summit.

Colour

Fifteen specialised workers to repaint the Eiffel Tower (May 1939).

Ways to protect the iron from rusting were studied from the moment of fabricating the first tower parts. Their slenderness, constant exposure to rain and pollution from numerous neighbourhood factories and mechanical deformation to which they were submitted had weakened them. A preliminary coat of oil-based paint, iron minium or red lead, was applied at the Atelier de Levallois, followed by a "rejuvenation" after assemblage to surfaces battered during manoeuvring and to the rivets. Établissements Nourrison recovered them with two additional coats of paint "of bright Venetian red-iron minium" and linseed oil. Then, from 15 March to 1 May, the same company laid down a fourth coat of "very thick, varnished paint". Guaranteed for one year, it was a dark brownish-red at the base which progressively lightened toward the summit.

In 1892, Eiffel judged it useful to "freshen up" the colour, this time to yellow-ochre. Then in 1899 the colour was toned down to yellowish-orange, dark at the base and clear yellow at the top. Painting campaigns followed every seven years, with an interruption in 1914. In 1924, the rusted sections were covered with a reddish-brown paint and the entirety in yellowish-brown, each campaign necessitating 50 tons of paint and 25,000 working hours.

Painters of the tower, colour engraving, 1900 (Paris, Private Collection).

The year 1968 was agitated at the Commission des Sites. Considering the tower's reddish-brown colour had become too "antiquated", diverse personalities militated in favour of a pale blue-grey in harmony with the Parisian sky. But, as is well-known, blue paints pose various problems; a reconciliation with the present grey-beige was consequently made.

**"Polishing up"
the Eiffel Tower**
in May 1939.

Illuminations during the 1900 Exposition, multi-colour engraving.

Lighting and illuminations

For the 1900 Exposition, gas burners from 1889 were replaced by 3,200 incandescent lamps and, seven years later, 6-metre high illuminated numbers indicated the hour at the second-level floor.

The Citroën Tower by night, 1925.
Fernando Jacopozzi engaged National Navy topmen and Paris firemen to mount 32km of heavy cable, 56km of lighter cable and wooden planks (10cm wide by 5cm thick) on which were affixed lighting devices and 200,000 light bulbs in six different colours (Paris, Citroën Collection).

However, it was a Florentine who brought about enchantment. Fernando Jacopozzi (1877-1932) had already executed several luminous devices (at Place de la Concorde, Place Vendôme, and the like) when he proposed to the committee of the Exposition des Arts décoratifs and industriels (previewed for 1925) an exorbitantly priced illumination project for the tower. Assuring himself of the necessary authorisations beforehand, by means of a 3-metre-high photograph pierced with holes to convey at least a notion of his concept, he next convinced automobile magnate André Citroën—rather easily—but late in the day.

At 10 o'clock on the evening of 4 July 1925, the tower was lit up like an immense torch, first along the arrises, then by a rain of blue stars, followed by enormous arabesques describing the signs of the Zodiac, a red flame at the tower coping, pylon-mounted shields with "1889" and "1925", great white stars, soon streaming and transforming into comets ... whose golden tails elongated, then enlarged to form the letters CITROËN, whilst within the shields the double chevron was substituted for the dates. In such a fashion, nine "tableaux" succeeded one another on the other three sides.

The entire production amounted to 500,000 francs at the current value. Success was immense and, from one extension to the next, publicity lingered on despite the cost which, with inflation, soon hovered around one million annually. Despite all, in 1933 Citroën requested that Jacopozzi insert a luminous clock with the letter "Ë"; the hour hands were multicoloured, the face measured 15 metres in diameter. At the end of 1934, the Citroën advertisement was extinguished, the company being obliged to go into voluntary liquidation before the Michelin take-over. In 1937, for the Exposition internationale des arts et techniques, the architect André Granet (1881-1974) executed a gigantic central light fixture on the first floor fashioned out of multi-coloured, 10-kilometre-long fluorescent tubing, whilst thirty projectors lit the interior with gold, blue, white, and red reflections. There were celebrations, fireworks, concerts: Ébert, Milhaud, Honegger, and many others composed music which was diffused in the tower.

Following double page | 45
Illuminations for the Exposition internationale des arts et des techniques of 1937, André Granet gouache (Paris, Musée d'Orsay, Eiffel Collection).

Granet's illuminations for the Exposition internationale des arts et des techniques of 1937. Frontal view of the tower (Paris, Institut français d'architecture, Granet Collection).

View from underneath the Eiffel Tower, illuminations by Granet for the 1937 Exposition (Paris, Institut français d'architecture, Granet Collection).

The tower on the night of 31 December 1985.
This new lighting was perfected to reduce electricity consumption and render the Eiffel Tower's metal structure more luminous and more present in the city (Lighting of the Eiffel Tower, SNTE/Pierre Bideau design).

Then came the blackout. At the end of World War II, a small beacon served to track aircraft. In June 1952, it was replaced on either side of a television set by two very wide-span beacons which remained in service until 1974. In April 1958, 1,290 projectors were installed in the hollowed trenches along the Champ-de-Mars gardens to illuminate the tower. This arrangement had three inconveniences: it was dull, hardly powerful despite its great energy consumption, and irritating (not to say blinding) to nocturnal visitors and restaurant clientele. Nonetheless, it functioned until 31 December 1985.

1889-1989: the Eiffel Tower at 100 years.
Illuminations for the centenary of the "odious column of bolted-down sheet metal", so decried by its adversaries and now a symbol of the French capital, participating in all its festivities and celebrations.

Wanting to modify the lighting, the Société nouvelle d'exploitation de la Tour called on consultants Sechaud and Bossuyt, who, with François Dhôtel, launched a competition, won by Pierre Bideau. The latter refined a solution after a series of tests effectuated in November 1984 with the aid of high-pressure sodium vapour lamps installed on the structure. What remained to be defined was the type of projector, the power of the lamps, and the most suitable sites in order to obtain greatest uniformity. To facilitate maintenance, all lamps were 1000-watts, except at the summit (200 and 400 watts). The in-

stallation of 192 projectors lasted three months, some alighting only a few metres, others up to 50 metres. Lighting arrangements were ready on 31 December 1985. The three-million-franc cost outlay was amortised over three years, and the new lighting unanimously appreciated.

For the year 2000, 20,000 light bulbs were in-

The tower as symbol.
According to a 1996 poll carried out in Germany, Spain, Great Britain, and Italy, more than half of the people questioned considered that the tower best represents Europe. The exception was the Germans, who prefer the Brandenburg Gate. In the late nineteenth century, frequentation wavered around 200,000 entries annually, then doubled in the 1920s, falling to 250,000-300,000 in the 1930s, with peaks of 1,000,000 in 1900, 600,000 in 1925, 800,000 in 1937. It surpassed one million from 1950, two million by 1964, three in 1973, four in 1984, six at present: one-quarter of the visitors come from France, half from other European countries, the last quarter from the rest of the world. The tower is the sole French historic monument not subsidised and profit-making (around 27 million francs), paid out to the City of Paris.

Pyrotechical ballet
for passage to the year 2000, created by Yves Pépin and Christophe Berthonneau, Production ECA2/Groupe F.

stalled to sparkle through the night during ten minutes at each fixed hour, except at one o'clock in the morning, when the tower glittered, and all other lights were extinguished.

Palais de l'Électricité, proposal to dress the Eiffel Tower for the Exposition of 1900 (Paris, Musée d'Orsay, Eiffel Collection).

Changes to the tower

Anticipating an affluence of visitors at the Exposition of 1900, the Roux & Combaluzier hydraulic lifts within the east and west piers were replaced by electric lifts furnished by Fives-Lille, to allow 20,000 rather than 18,000 persons to be transported during the 10-hour day. The Otis lift in the north pier was enlarged and its speed accelerated, that in the south pier eliminated, and its staircase to the second floor enlarged.

Refurbishing project for the tower (not executed) for the Universal Exposition of 1900, Sauvestre watercolour (Paris, Collection Tour Eiffel).

In 1937, André Granet (who had married Eiffel's grandaughter) proceeded with a controversial modernisation plan for the tower. The first-floor pavilions, covered with small, Art-Nouveau-type wooden vaults, were demolished, making way for panoramic restaurants recovered with a uniform, horizontal slab, undoubtedly more in keeping with current tastes, supported by simple geometric forms such as those at the Palais de Chaillot. These forms did not interfere with the lines of the four truss rafters which gave the tower its elan and stability. A similar intervention at the second floor would have less severe consequences.

From one extension to the next, the society created by Eiffel in 1888 came to the end of the terms of its contract in 1979. Estimating that it did not sufficiently fulfil its

obligations vis-à-vis the ever-increasing visitors, the City of Paris did not renew its concession which it had granted to the Société nouvelle d'exploitation de la tour Eiffel out of which it reserved for itself 30 per cent of the capital, the remaining 70 per cent going to SAGI, a major real estate company of which the City held 40 per cent of its capital. During the course of many years, some constructions had been added one after another, so much so that the first storey supported a surcharge of 1,120 tons. That had to be completely eliminated and the deformed structures reinforced or replaced. Three new rooms were built along the plans of François Dhôtel to house a restaurant, souvenir shop, Gustave Eiffel Room, post office, and Cinémax. In its desire to appear neutral, this architecture provoked some friction with the Direction de l'Architecture [Architecture Administration], the tower having become classified as an historic monument on 24 June 1964.

In 1982, the second storey was in its turn refurbished as the Jules Verne Restaurant. The spiral staircase linking the second level to the summit was replaced by two straight-run staircases and the Édoux double lift car by Otis electric cars, replaced in their turn in 1994 and 1995. A goods lift was installed in 1989 to reserve the other lifts exclusively for visitors.

New lifts: 65 per cent of tower expenses go to maintenance costs and personnel; 85 per cent of its revenues is assured by entry fees.

La Tour Eiffel, by Georges Seurat (1859-1891), oil on canvas, 1889 (San Francisco, Fine Arts Museum).

The tower and the plastic arts

Painters and sculptors have long taken interest in the tower: a small painting by Georges Seurat dated 1889, thirty-six lithographs by Henri Rivière, episodic appearances in works by the Douanier Rousseau, some pictures by Marc Chagall, Raoul Dufy, and others. Robert Delaunay was the first artist to discover the tower, in 1910. More than a subject of mere study, the tower became his pretext to study light and space which led him to explode its structures and open the way to abstraction. The

Opposite page
La Tour Eiffel, by Robert Delaunay, oil on canvas, 1928 (Paris, Musée national d'Art moderne).

Bonjour Paris, by Marc Chagall, oil on cardboard, circa 1939-1942 (Basel, Private Collection).

tower was the first work to delimit space without enclosing it, and Delaunay the first artist to perceive this spatial phenomenon, visible simultaneously from within and without. Arriving in Paris in 1911 and 1913, sculptors Antoine Pevsner and Naum Gabo picked up lessons from the tower. By

La Tour Eiffel, by Nicolas de Staël, oil on canvas (Troyes, Musée d'Art moderne).

La Tête construite, by Naum Gabo, sculpture, 1916.

1916, Gabo's *La Tête construite [Constructed Head]* broke with traditional sculpture, at least on two points: it is no longer determined either by volumes or by solids; it alone determines space which becomes the integral part of the work. Pevsner recognized the tower's importance. So did Vladimir Tatlin, as recalled in his 1919-1920 Memorial to the Third International [after his 1913 Paris visit]: "Eiffel was the first constructivist".

Visit

Surroundings

The tower dominates the Champ-de-Mars, exercise grounds for pupils of the adjacent École Militaire [French Military Academy] constructed by Ange-Jacques Gabriel in 1773. When the tower was erected, the grounds still stretched along the Avenue de La Bourdonnais to the east and the Avenue de Suffren to the west. Reduced from 44 to 24 hectares by housing estates, they were redesigned into a public garden from 1908, after architect Jean-Camille Formigé's designs.

On the opposite right bank of the Seine, the Palais de Chaillot from the 1937 Exposition (built on the plans of Léon Azéma, Charles Boileau, and Jacques Carlu) replaced a palace designed by Gustave Davioud and Jules Bourdais for the Exposition of 1878. Practically at the tower base, the Pont d'Iéna was constructed by Corneille Lamandé in 1811, but it was necessary to wait until 1853 for its pedestals to receive their prescribed equestrian statues and pier tympanums to be ornamented with Antoine-Louis Bayre's Imperial eagles. Judged too narrow when completed, the bridge width was tripled (35 metres between parapets) from 1934 to 1937, in light of the exposition.

Four piers

The Champ-de-Mars axis being set at 45° to the meridian of Paris, the **four piers** of the tower stand on axis to the four cardinal points. Access to the Eiffel tower is made through one of the four piers. Before, it was advised to visit the lift machinery beneath the east and west pier bases. These lifts constructed by Fives-Lille were installed in 1899 in anticipation of the Exposition of 1900; they are hydraulic lifts that pistons hoist by a system of pulley-block cables from the ground level to the first floor.

At the foot of the north pier, the **bust of Gustave Eiffel** was achieved with subscription monies raised by General Ferrié. Inaugurated on 2 May 1929, it was sculpted by Antoine Bourdelle, with a pedestal designed by Auguste Perret and André Granet.

First floor

At the first-floor level, 57 metres above ground, the principal attraction resides essentially in the different views afforded over Paris. But one should also not miss:

- at the north pillar, the observatory of summit fluctuations in which a laser beam directly retraces oscillations described by the Eiffel Tower summit in reaction to solar heat and wind force. It is the sun rather than the wind which actually moves the tower to a greater degree. Gusts of 214 km/hr were registered at the summit during the violent storm of 26 December 1999, resulting in a displacement of 9 centimetres. As truss rafters in the shade dilate less than those exposed to the sun, the tower can theoretically retract from the sun's impact by 18 centimetres. In fact, the maximum effect of 15 centimetres was registered on 16 January 1971.

Further to the west, one finds the **Altitude 95 Restaurant.** In 1889, there had already existed several restaurants on the tower's first platform: French (facing the École Militaire), Russian, Flemish (later transformed into a theatre), and an Anglo-American bar;

- at the west pillar, the **Feroscope** [Ironscope], a transparent bubble within which is placed a tower beam painted with diverse coloured paint samples dating from the origi-

nal red. In addition to pigments, these paints were always linseed oil-based, then combined linseed oil and China wood. Whatever their colour, these paints provided the basic conservation element for the tower. That treatment was the sole guarantee of durability. Interactive videos facilitate the discovery of construction assemblage techniques, riveting, and painting protection work. Heading southward, one finds a buffet, souvenir shop, post office (where, amongst other services, postage stamps are cancelled with the special "Paris-Tour Eiffel" tampon), and the **General Ferrié Room** where static and

moving images are mounted, recalling the great events of the monument. On the first floor of this room, one can see a hologram of the tower, the remainder of the floor being occupied by another room for temporary exhibitions;

- at the south pillar is displayed a **section of the original staircase** which linked the second and third floors. It was replaced by two straight-run staircases which, from 1983, left the centre of the tower to two double car lifts. Twenty staircase sections were dispersed in an international auction sale, retransmitted by twenty-one television stations;

- at the east pillar figures the **hydraulic pump** whose pressure activates the piston for the lift connecting the second and third floors. Close to the north pier, the Gustave Eiffel Room accommodates meetings and conferences.

Second floor

Here one is situated 115 metres above the ground. On the interior platform, toward the west pillar, a glass-covered orifice affords a view onto the **"gouffre"** or **"abyss"**, a name given to the central void beneath the tower. Next to it, the Visitors' Galaxy offers the possibility to participate in the construction of a virtual tower formed by millions of stars, each born from the arrival of every visitor. With the aid of Alias, a small robot, the visitor can fly through the galaxy of the Eiffel Tower, engrave one's initials on a star of "one's own", and later locate oneself on the Internet. Panels detail the lift functions, and a buffet offers a refreshment service. Boutiques provide souvenirs. Other shops occupy the upper platform where entry to the Jules Verne Restaurant is situated and through which the south pillar can also be reached. In 1889, other than restaurants and boutiques, the second floor offered other notable attractions: a print shop installed by the daily newspaper *Le Figaro* where the day's newspaper was fabricated regularly, a veritable certificate of ascension carrying the purchaser's name. In 1900, and right up until 1914, it was on this floor that, each day at noon, a **canon**

marked the hour for Parisians. In 1907, a giant clock was placed at the same level, with its illuminated, 6-metre-high numbers. On the second platform, too, Eiffel fitted out his aerodynamics laboratory in 1903, dedicated to research on gravity.

Wounded by critics who denounced the tower's lack of purpose, Eiffel wanted to dedicate it to science, having the names of seventy-two French intellectuals (who had distinguished themselves since 1789) painted in gold letters around the second-floor gallery. Thus, there one can read the names of Ampère, Chaptal, Gay-Lussac, and Lavoisier, as well as those of engineers, such as Flachat and Seguin. From this second-floor platform, one can reach the lifts to the third floor.

Third and fourth floors

Some panoramic tables are disposed in a glass gallery; they indicate major Parisian sites and point out the direction and distances of the largest cities in the world. In clear weather, devoid of pollution, the view was reported to extend 90 kilometres. An open-air staircase leads to the fourth floor where one can see a small room, refurbished to represent the **salon** where Eiffel, in the company of his eldest daughter, Claire Salles, encountered Thomas Edison during the Exposition of 1889, an event perpetuated by the installation there of three wax figures. A plaque recalls the first radiophonic transmission launched from this floor. A fifth floor houses the lift pulleys and a part of Télédiffusion de France installations which occupy most of the sixth floor. These latter two floors are closed to visitors.

60 | **One hundred years of urban evolution seen from the Eiffel Tower.**

What visitors saw at the beginning of the nineteenth century ... *(right)*

... and at the crest of the third millennium *(opposite page).*

In one century, the city has grown more dense, especially around the periphery. Its boundaries, merged into the suburbs, are no longer perceptible. The belt of high-rise towers immure not only Paris (which no longer murmurs), but encompass part of the suburbs, notably at La Défense.

Facing south[1]. | 61
Following a highly controversial decision of the Municipal Council in December 1903, the Champ-de-Mars was reduced from 44 to 24 hectares. (Where then would the dirigibles land?) Beyond the École Militaire, the Tour Montparnasse rears up (1973).

Facing west[2].
From the Cail metallurgy factories and the Menier telephone cable-manufacturing plant followed the Beaugrenelle Towers (to the left) after the 1960s-1970s, based on a project by Lopez, Pottier, and Proux. As for the village of Auteuil, it became an entirely separate quarter of Paris (to the right).

Facing east[3].
Towards the centre of the city, greenery is rare, constructions have gained height, to the extent of masking Montmartre.

Facing north[4].
The Palais de Trocadéro of Davioud and Bourdet for the Exposition of 1878 became the Palais de Chaillot of Boileau, Carlu, and Azéma for the 1937 fair. Countryside made way for the city. In the distance, the high-rise towers of La Défense.

Tower statistics

- Original height: 300.65m
- Height since 1957: 320.75m
- Height to 1st floor: 57.63m; surface area: 4,200m^2
- Height to 2nd floor: 115.73m; surface area: 1,400m^2
- Height to 3rd floor: 276.13m; surface area: 350m^2
- Square base of 129.22m on each side
- Weight of the tower alone: 7,000 tons
- All the iron of the tower melted down in a uniform plaque to the base dimensions would form a thickness of 6cm
- 50 tons of paint and 20,000 hours of work are required to resurface the tower every seven years
- The tower necessitated more than 1,700 drawings for the ensemble and 3,629 working drawings, each 100 x 80cm; their surface area exceeds 4,000m^2
- Duration of ground work, foundations and masonry: five months and four days (exactly fifty-four days)
- Duration of assemblage work: twenty-one months (exactly 339 days), with a team that never exceeded 210 persons; 121 workers on the site to raise the tower, 326 within the Eiffel firm.
  Total duration: two years, two months, five days
- 18,000 different pieces assembled with 2,500,000 rivets, of which 1,050,846 were mounted on the construction site
- 1,665 steps
- fourty-eight surveillance cameras

The tallest monuments

circa 2600 B.C. Pyramid of Cheops (Egypt): 146m
128 A.D. Hadrian's Pantheon (Rome): 43.50m
537 Hagia Sophia (Constantinople): 55m
circa 1230 Cathedral of Notre-Dame (Paris): 66m
1439 Cathedral of Notre-Dame spire (Strasbourg): 142m
circa 1575 Saint Peter's Basilica cupola (Rome): 132m
1706 Church of Les Invalides dome (Paris): 105m
1710 Saint Paul's Cathedral (London): 110m
1812 The Pantheon (Paris): 83m
1880 Saint Materne Cathedral spire (Cologne): 159m
1888 Washington Monument (D.C.): 169.25m
1889 Eiffel Tower (Paris): 300m
1900 La Mole Antonelliana (Turin): 168m
1930 Chrysler Building (New York): 318m
1931 Empire State Building (New York): 378m

(Years indicated refer to date of construction termination.)

Where the Whole World Meets

In 1954, a television mast reached 479m in Oklahoma City (United States). It was followed by around twenty others, all exceeding 300m. Regarding towers, the International Federation of Great Towers of the World cites the CN Tower (Toronto) at 553m and the Ostankino Tower (Moscow) at 540m.

The Eiffel Tower and major monuments of the world in 1889 (Paris, Collection Tour Eiffel).

Empire State Building, 1938.

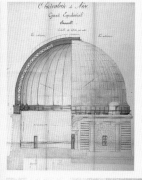

Works constructed by Gustave Eiffel in France

Agen: train station concourse (1865)
Bayonne: railway bridge over the Nive (1863)
Bergerac: railway bridge over the Dordogne (1882), transformed into the "Pont de Gillets", transport bridge
Bordeaux: railway bridge over the Garonne (1860)
Cazères-sur-Adour: transport bridge over the Adour (1880)
Charenton: railway bridge over the Marne (1883), now supporting two central roads
Chinon: railway bridge over the Vienne (1874)
Cubzac: road bridge, National 10 autoroute, over the Dordogne (1883)
Évaux: "La Tarde" railway viaduct (1885)
Garabit: railway viaduct over the Truyère (1884), 16 km south of Saint-Flour
Monistrol-d'Allier: road bridge over the Allier (1888)
Montréjeau: Sarrieu railway bridge over the Garonne (1878)
Nice: observatory cupola, great coast road (1886)
Paris fourth district: synagogue, n° 21, Rue des Tournelles (1876)
Paris sixth district: Church of Notre-Dame-des-Champs structure, n° 91, Boulevard du Montparnasse (1876)
Paris seventh district: Le Bon Marché Department Store, n° 22, Rue de Sèvres (1879)
Paris seventeenth district: Lycée Carnot gymnasium, n° 145, Boulevard Malesherbes (1876)
Péault: bridge road over the Lay (1878)
Saint-Bonnet-de-Rochefort: Neuvial (1868) and Rouzat (1869) railway viaducts over the Sioule
Saint-Laurent-sur-Sèvre: bridge road over the Sèvre (1879)
Sarrieu: see Montréjeau above
Sioule: see Saint-Bonnet above
Tardes: see Évaux above
Thouars: railway viaduct over the Thouet (1873)
Toulouse: station concourse (1865), a section of the present station
Valentine: railway bridge over the Garonne (1878)
Vivario: "Vecchio" railway bridge (1890)

A short bibliography

On Eiffel

Lemoine (Bertrand),
Gustave Eiffel,
Paris, Hazan, 1984.
Marrey (Bernard),
*La Vie et l'Œuvre
extraordinaires de
Monsieur Gustave Eiffel,*
Paris, Graphite, 1984.
Poncetton (François),
Eiffel, le magicien du fer,
Paris, La Tournelle, 1939.
Prévost (Jean),
Eiffel, Paris, Rieder, 1929.

On the Eiffel Tower

Barthes (Roland),
photos by André Martin,
La Tour Eiffel,
Paris, Delpire, 1964.
Braibant (Charles),
Histoire de la tour Eiffel,
Paris, Plon, 1964.
Bure (Charles de),
La Tour de 300 mètres,
Lausanne, André Delcour, 1988.
Lamberini (Daniela) and
Manno Tolu (Rosalia),
*De la Toscane à l'Europe
de Gustave Eiffel,*
Livourne, Sillabe, 1999.
Landon (François),
La Tour Eiffel,
Paris, Ramsay, 1981.
Lemoine (Bertrand),
La Tour de Monsieur Eiffel,
Paris, Gallimard, "Découvertes"
collection, 1989.

Captions

Cover
1st: pyrotechnical ballet
for the passage into the year
2000, created by Yves Pépin
and Christophe Berthonneau,
Production ECA2/Groupe
F. Eiffel Tower lighting,
© SNTE/Pierre Bideau
conception.
4th: Eiffel bust by Antoine
Bourdelle, north pillar base.
1st exterior overleaf:
Gustave Eiffel at the Tower
summit, 1889 (Paris,
Collection Tour Eiffel).
2nd exterior overleaf: detail
of the tower metal frame.
Page 1
1t: inauguration medal of the
tower, 6 May 1889 (Paris,
Musée Gustave Moreau);
1c: view of the Eiffel Tower;
1b: Gustave Eiffel (Paris,
Collection Tour Eiffel).
Chronology
From left to right
and from top to bottom:
- Metal construction:
Crystal Palace, constructed
for the London Universal
Exhibition of 1851, English
watercolour, second half of
the 19th century (Paris,
Bibliothèque des Arts
décoratifs/J.-L. Charmet);
new Reading Room,
Bibliothèque impériale,
L'Illustration, May 1868
(*L'Illustration*/Keystone);
Viaduc de Garabit (see
p.10t); view of the bridge on
the Firth of Forth, Scotland,
December 1888
(*L'Illustration*/Keystone).
- Politics: Napoleon III, 1855;
Third Republic, 1878
(Malécot Coll.;
P.Cadet/CMN reprod.);
Wilhelm II, inauguration
medal of Upper Koenigsburg
castle restoration, 1908
(Upper-Koenigsburg Coll.);
inauguration of the Paris
Universal Exposition,
14 April 1900 (Collection
Tour Eiffel/SNTE).
- Culture: Victor Hugo,
Émile Zola by Nadar (Paris,
Médiathèque de
l'architecture et du
patrimoine, Archives
photographiques).
- Science and technology:
Texas oil wells, nineteenth
century, engraving (DR);
Graham Bell, Édouard
Branly, engravings (DR);
Santos-Dumont in a dirigible
(see p. 38b).

BnF: Bibliothèque
nationale de France, Paris.
CMN: Centre des
monuments nationaux, Paris.
IFA: Institut français
d'architecture, Paris.
RMN: Réunion des musées
nationaux, Paris.
SNTE: Société nouvelle
d'exploitation de la tour Eiffel.

Photographic credits
© ADAGP, Paris 2001: 8t,
25, 52t and c; AKG Photos
Paris: 51b, 52t; BnF: 30b;
CMN/F. Charafi: 19, 26b, 54;
CMN/W. Korsak: 4th cover,
1c, 41b, 48t, 49t, 51t and c,
55t and c, 56, 57, 58t and c,
59, 61, 62t and tc; CMN/I.
Revault: 4t; CMN/C. Rose:
55b; CMN/N. Vu Dinh: 48b;
J.-L. Charmet: 44t, 62b, 63t
rt; Tour Eiffel Coll./SNTE:
1st exterior overleaf, 1b, 2-
3,6t, 8b, 9, 10, 11, 13, 14, 18,
20t and c, 21, 22-23 (except
22 tc, bc and b), 24, 27t, 29,
32c and b, 33rt, 34b rt, 37b,
38, 39t, 40t, 61c, 50b, 58b,
63b rt; SNTE/P. Bideau
design: 48, 49; priv. coll./B.
Marrey: 20b, 26b, 27c, 34c
left, 39b, 42b, 50b, 52b
(DR), 59c, 62bc, 63t left,
63b rt; Citroën Coll.: 44c
and b; Dagli Orti: 7t;
IFA/DAF: 45; Groupe F/J.-P.
Delagarde/X. Filly/T. Nava:
1st cover, 49b;
L'Illustration/Keystone: 4b,
5, 17, 22tc, 28, 32b, 33bc,
39t, 42t, 43, 53;
© L & M Services B.V.
Amsterdam 20010114: 53;
RMN: 36; RMN/Schormans:
35; RMN/R.G. Ojeda: 1b;
RMN/G. Blot: 7b, 52c;
RMN/Hervé: 8t; RMN/P.
Néri: 25; RMN/C. Jean: 33c,
46-47, 50t; Roger-Viollet:
6b, 12, 15, 16, 22bc and b,
30t, 31, 32t, 34t, 40b, 60.

Collection director
Alix Sallé
Coordinating editor
Michèle Decré-Cyssau
Documents coordinator
Françoise Arnault
Translator
Barbara Shapiro Comte
Copy editor
Elizabeth Ayre
Graphics
Jean-Philippe Guillerme
Design
Atalante/Paris
Graphic design
encore/Paris
Production coordinator
Carine Merse
Photoengraving
**Scann'Ouest/
La Chapelle-sur-Erdre**
Printing
Néo-Typo/Besançon

© Centre des monuments
nationaux/Monum, Éditions
du patrimoine, Paris 2001

Dépôt légal: June 2001